THE FLOWER SHOP

CHRISTMAS

By Sally Page

Additional photography by Billy Kelly, Alex Page and Jake Oliver

THE FLOWER SHOP

Published by Half Full Press

Published 2007 by Half Full Press
1814 Franklin Street, Suite 440
Oakland, CA 94612
(800) 841-0873
(510) 839-5471

Printed and bound in China by C&C Offset Printing

ISBN: 0-9719552-8-X
ISBN: 978-0-9719552-8-8

Also by Sally Page: The Flower Shop - A Year in the Life of a Country Flower Shop

For more information visit www.halffullpress.com
www.tedmartinflowers.com

This book is for Alex and Libby

*"There be none of Beauty's daughters
With a magic like thee"*

Introduction

Christmas comes slowly to the village of Tisbury, creeping in with the early morning mists and with the frosts that dust the surrounding countryside in shimmering silver.

Winter settles into the valley and the days in the flower shop are busy and convivial as we help prepare for celebrations and homecomings.

The following pages are a record of this flower shop Christmas. It is a rolling, country road of a journal that meanders through the life of the shop, stopping along the way to visit friends and neighbours from the village. These people are kind enough to invite us into their homes to share their festivities. We would like to thank them for their warm hospitality.

The days are short now and travelling home in the evening there is the faint smell of wood smoke in the chilly air. Since I was a child I have loved these early evenings; a world of half-drawn curtains through which you glimpse homes lit by the glow of lamps and firelight.

*"How bittersweet it is, on winter's night,
To listen, by the spluttering, smoking fire,
As distant memories, through the fog-dimmed light,
Rise, to the muffled chime of churchbell choir."*
Charles Baudelaire

So, draw your chair a little closer to the fire, settle a glass of something warming near at hand and enjoy, with us, Christmas in an English country flower shop.

On the First Day of Christmas

"With faint dry sound,
Like steps of passing ghosts,
The leaves, frost-crisp'd, break from the trees
And fall."
Adelaide Crapsey

Then Comes the Winter

Brown and yellow lacy leaves curl and crackle underfoot on the doorstep of Ted Martin Flowers. They have been blown there by the sharp east wind that is catching at my coat as I pocket my car keys and turn towards the door. It is as if the wind is in a hurry for me to get my coat off and start work.

Opening the door it seems like the colours of the leaves have been blown in with me. The banks of flowers are bright and autumnal against the cream painted walls and on the table in the centre of the shop there is a splash of red berries, which gives a sense that Christmas is not that far away.

"He draws and draws his slender threads of sound
Between the dark boughs and the freezing ground"
Anthony Rye

Inside the shop Ted is unpacking a box of golden alstromeria, the petals of which are flecked a leathery brown. She places them in an enamel bucket on the table, alongside terracotta roses and bunches of rosemary. I can hear Jennifer in the back making tea and I think I can just catch the smell of croissants. As I have forgotten to eat breakfast I really hope that she has brought some to work with her.

The phone starts to ring and we are soon busy making up bouquets for deliveries. One is for a local lady who has just received the all-clear from cancer. Her friends and family are understandably delighted, as are we. During her long treatment we have sent a number of arrangements to her from well-wishers.

One of the customers in from the biting wind spends a great deal of time examining the range of flowers in the shop. She and her family had a flower farm in Africa and many of the varieties that we stock are familiar to her. She talks to me about the fields of sunflowers they used to grow and of her sadness at losing the farm because of political unrest.

Jenny

As the shop is getting busier and busier Ted decides to take on another part-time member of staff. Like all of us, Jenny has come to work with flowers by a circuitous route. As a young girl she had a job in a florist working Saturdays, but later went on to travel and to work in mental health. She always kept up her interest in flowers and has now decided that she would once again like to have a job in a flower shop. When Ted interviews her she recognises her as one of the very first brides she prepared wedding flowers for. It is not long before she has joined us and Jennifer has worked out exactly how Jenny likes her tea (green tea without milk).

Jenny is gentle, cheerful and very helpful and we are all pleased to have her with us, but Jennifer especially so. Not everyone realises, but Jennifer really dislikes being called 'Jenny'. Now with our own Jenny around it is easy to insist everyone calls her 'Jennifer'.

Winter Colouring
My father drew the sky in pencil,
B for the flat cold clouds,
H for the hard horizon of trees.
But I pulled the crayons from his pot,
Added crimson for his scarf and nose,
Pressed hard for the conker in his glove,
And left shavings on his desk like leaves.

A new delivery of pottery arrives in the shop ready for Christmas. It is hand-made by a lady called Jane Hogben who works from her pottery on a farm about an hour or so from here. I particularly like the robins that look as if they have just hopped onto the mugs and planters.

The church down the road from the shop is holding a coffee morning and I have brought in a coffee cake to add to the cake sale. I love coffee cake and Ted, knowing this, nips out of the shop and buys it for us in the sale. This is just as well, as when I proudly cut into it I find I have forgotten to remove the baking paper from the bottom of each layer. After a lot of dissecting and peeling we each have a pile of cake to go with our coffee.

During the day a regular customer, Mr Little, comes in to order some flowers. He is shortly followed by a new customer, Mrs Large. I can't help smiling and thinking they should really swap names since Mrs Large is very petite and Mr Little is a tall, broad-shouldered man.

flower shop secrets
ARRANGEMENTS

Sometimes customers bring in containers they would like us to re-use, including the Oasis that is inside. We are always happy to use the container but would never re-use the Oasis. The reason for this is that the previously formed holes and indentations can create air holes that stop the new flowers from drinking.

For the same reason, when working with new Oasis you need to be careful not to push the stems in too far so they have to be withdrawn as you adjust them. This can also form air pockets around the stems.

Smokey winter nights

Driving home, the sky looks like a bonfire that has been set alight by the sinking sun. Turning the corner on a back lane, I see wisps of smoke from a pile of leaves being burnt on the edge of a copse, the smoke mingling with the colours of the flaming sky.

"Look, how those steep woods on the mountain's face
Burn, burn against the sunset; now the cold
Invades our very noon: the year's grown old"
Hilaire Belloc

Sally's Coffee Cake

I could never make my cakes look like they do in magazines and then it occurred to me that if I added more ingredients and used a narrow tin, the cake would have to be tall and fat and impressive! So this is what I now do.

I use two tins that are only 7 inches across but are 2 inches deep. My recipe is based on, 3 eggs, 6 oz of self raising flour, 6 oz of caster sugar, 6 oz of butter and a teaspoon of baking powder. I put all the ingredients in a bowl, add a splash of milk and beat them together using an electric whisk. I then add some strong black instant coffee.

Cook for around 30 minutes at gas mark 3, 325°f (170°c), or until the cake bounces back when pressed. And as long as you remember to remove the baking paper on the bottom before you ice the cake, you cannot fail to look good.

On the Second Day of Christmas

"Roger the Dutchman" arrives in his huge truck, filling the space outside the shop and temporarily cutting out all the natural light. Ted climbs inside and starts to choose wraps of lilies, roses, cabbages, hypericum and lisianthus. Jennifer pokes her head into the lorry with a mug of coffee for Roger and to remind Ted we need some gold-coloured roses for a golden wedding anniversary.

Roger and Ted carry the armfuls of flowers into the shop, Roger frowning and shaking his head at the music we have playing in the background. He once lent us his favourite CD and when we listened to it, it was clear that we were never going to agree on music. The customer I am serving disagrees with him. She says she likes the music, especially as she hasn't heard the song for such a long time. She laughs and tells us, "The last time I heard this I had a waist!"

Running to see the truck arrive

20

The shop closes at lunch-time on Saturdays, but a bride and bridesmaid still have to be seen. Jennifer and Ted often invite brides to come in after the shop has shut so they can talk through ideas in peace and quiet.

Rosie, our Saturday girl, carries flowers down to the hairdressers. They have been ordered for a favourite client who is having her hair done for her birthday party that evening. Sue from the hairdressers was in the shop early this morning placing the order and choosing the colours she thought the lady would like.

Winter planting

With Christmas approaching we order trays and trays of bulbs, such as hyacinths, for planting up in baskets, buckets and trugs. These, and the other plants we stock, make popular presents. One customer, James, comes in and chooses a planted basket as a gift for friends they are going to stay with. We notice he is moving slowly around the shop and he explains that he played in the Dads' football team for the local primary school the night before and that now he can barely walk.

"All kindly tended gardens love December days,
And spread their latest riches out In winter's praise."
Dollie Radford

flower shop secrets
HYACINTHS

To keep hyacinths growing straight ensure they have plenty of all-round light. If they are tucked in a dark corner they tend to grow too fast towards a bright spot. All hyacinths, once they are blooming, may get top heavy and bend but this is easy to fix by taking a chopstick from the kitchen drawer and lightly tying the plant to it.

Once the flowers are over, hyacinths can be planted in the garden for the following year and over time you can watch them naturalise back to bluebells.

Jennifer chalks a letter on the pot so we know what colour the flowers will be

23

Visiting the Pottery

In the shop we sell Burleigh earthenware and just before Christmas I travel to Stoke on Trent to visit their pottery and to collect new samples. Middleport is an immense Victorian factory built in the 1880s alongside a canal that was used to bring the clay in from the West Country and take the finished china all over the empire. With many of the original presses and machines it is the only pottery in the world still producing china in very much the original way.

Yet a few years ago it looked like the factory would shut and the buildings would be bulldozed to make space for a car park. At that time, William and Rosemary Dorling made a final trip to the factory from their china shop in Hampshire. They drove up in a van intending to fill it with the last of the Burleigh ware. Before they left Middleport they had decided to mortgage their house and to try and save the factory.

The sale went ahead and Rosemary and William moved in, sleeping on camp-beds on the general office floor. At that time, they did not have enough money to pay their eighteen members of staff, so they opened up the order book and called all their customers, from Harrods to the smallest gift shop, and asked them if they would pay in advance. They all agreed. Eight years on the factory employs nearly seventy staff and their china is still sold all over the world.

The factory is fired by a boiler that was rescued from the middle of a Scottish field. It was discovered that this boiler had started its working life onboard HMS Liverpool.

Rosemary tells me that when walking through the factory gates she often gets a sense of the hundreds of workers who used to stream through at the end of each day. And up in the rooms above the general office it is said you can still sometimes smell the cigar smoke of Edmund Leigh, one of the original founders.

Rosemary has boxed up some samples for me to take back to Ted

During my visit John the mould-maker shows me the attic where all the Burleigh moulds, dating back to the late 1800s, are stored. He has catalogued many of them but is still unearthing hidden treasures wrapped in the original newspapers of the day.

Wandering through the rows of chalky moulds I spot designs for beautiful honeycombed art deco jugs, Churchill memorial mugs and commemorative plates from the World Wars.

The Burleigh patterns are transferred by hand as tissue paper is wrapped around the biscuitware.

The original press with hand-engraved plates prints the pattern onto the tissue paper.

"Move him into the sun –
Gently its touch awoke him once,
At home, whispering of fields unsown."
Wilfred Owen

After walking round the factory we stop for coffee and sandwiches by the fire in the factory shop. William Dorling has just brought in the Christmas tree and is busy wiring up the lights.

Angela, the shop manager, chats to us as she decorates oranges with cloves ready for the Christmas display. Like all the staff I have met she is warm and welcoming and looking around at the beautiful shop it is clear that she loves the china she sells.

Angela's Candles

This is an attractive, easy idea that I saw in the Burleigh factory shop. Angela, the shop manager, had placed a pillar candle on a Christmas ham stand, around which she had piled cranberries.

In one display she had placed sprigs of rosemary amongst the berries and in another, fresh bay leaves. Cinnamon sticks can also be arranged around the base of the candle to give more texture and fragrance.

On the Third Day
of Christmas

All the Christmas stock is now brought down from the storeroom that is situated around the corner from the shop. It takes several trips with a wobbly wheelbarrow to collect all the baskets, pine cones, boxes of ribbons and decorations.

A brother and sister visit the shop to discuss their parents' golden wedding anniversary. They bring with them a picture taken on the wedding day. As a surprise gift they would like us to recreate the wedding bouquet of freesias and roses, so they can present it to them at the celebrations.

Another couple is also organising a party, this time a Christmas supper party for friends returning from overseas. The customer explains to us that, as she is "as creative as a stone", she would like us to co-ordinate all the flowers for her. We suggest table centres based upon twig wreaths with hurricane lamps, vibernum and hyacinths.

A local business man comes in to buy flowers for a family friend – she is just back from Korea where she was acting as an advisor for the British government. He says she is rarely in as she has such a busy life, so a plant may be a better gift as it can easily be left. He tells us what an amazing woman she is, explaining that she didn't find time to write her first book until she was ninety!

Advent

I call around to see the Bickersteths and to deliver an advent wreath. Rosemary is hanging the first of the Christmas cards and John is at the dining room table, with a very antique looking address book, writing theirs.

"Still I love thee without art, Ancient person of my heart"
John Wilmot

I know that whenever I visit the Bickersteths I am assured of good coffee, tasty biscuits and John's entertaining stories.

When John retired from the Church he realised that, for the first time ever, there were three generations of the Queen's ecclesiastical household, past and present, still alive – himself included. He recounts how he cheekily wrote to ask the Queen if she would consider hosting a drinks party to mark this circumstance. The Queen's response was that she would do better than that and she invited the clergymen and their wives to Buckingham Palace for lunch.

John recalls that a few moments before the photograph, that is hung on his study wall, was taken, the Queen had chased nine corgies out of the room.

When my daughters were toddlers I made a string of advent stockings for them. Now as teenagers they are still keen to hunt in the Christmas box for the old tin we store them in. Each year it is just as exciting and each year, as I search for tiny gifts to put in them, I wish I had made them bigger!

Advent Calendars
I've found presents and stars,
Crackers and bows,
Snowmen and puddings,
And candles a-glow.
I've had candy and drums,
Trumpets and holly,
Colourful sweets,
A ted and a dolly.
I've seen stockings and bells,
A jolly Yule log,
But I still haven't found
A pig or a frog.

Work Experience in the Flower Shop

Every year local schools send pupils out for a day's work experience. My daughter, Libby, and her friend, Alice, decide they would like to do their day's work experience in the flower shop. They are very excited about coming in and have a wonderful time sorting the flowers, running errands and unpacking parcels of new Christmas stock.

This is a sad and difficult day for Ted as it is the anniversary of her father's death. Yet she is pleased to have the girls in as their giggling and chatting has helped to distract her. She says she never knew that using a pricing gun could be so much fun.

Step by Step

These arrangements look pretty lined up on a shelf or mantelpiece and they are very easy to make.

Step 1: Scrub the cobwebs from some old flower pots and fill with left over pieces of wet or dry Oasis.

Step 2: Dig a hole in the Oasis to wedge a candle in and cover the Oasis that can still be seen with moss.

Step 3: To make a bow, fold the ribbon as shown and bend and twist a piece of florist's wire to hold it in place.

Step 4: Cut the wire to the right length and poke it down the side of the Oasis to position the bow against the pot.

We are contacted by a lady in America who would like to send some poinsettias to a convent in London. We select twelve large, English-grown plants and box them up ready for delivery. She wishes to give the Sisters these festive plants to help decorate their chapel for Christmas.

flower shop secrets
POINSETTIAS

If you have managed to keep a poinsettia plant going from last Christmas it is likely that the leaves are now green. The way to get them to turn red again is to keep the plant in the dark for a few weeks prior to Christmas.

My First Christmas Tree

Sheira's Sloe Gin

We are chatting about how difficult it is to find presents for men when Ted tells us about her friend Sheira's great idea. She buys interesting old decanters from charity shops and then fills them with home-made sloe gin.

To make sloe gin, collect your sloes from the blackthorn tree, wash them and remove their stems. It is best to collect the sloes after the first frost but if this is not possible put them in the freezer overnight.

Prick the sloes with a needle and put them in an old jar or bottle with half their weight of sugar. Then add the gin – you are aiming for the container to be roughly half-full of gin and half-full of sugary sloes.

Store the mixture in a dark cool place, shaking the jar every other day for a week and then once a week for six to eight weeks. When it is ready pour through a fine meshed sieve or muslin.

On the Fourth Day of Christmas

We start to prepare garlands and wreaths for Christmas; some we will sell in the shop whilst others have been specially ordered for customers' homes.

As I am working on a wreath Jennifer comes around the edge of the counter and whispers in my ear. Looking out into the shop I see a smartly dressed man wearing his bedroom slippers. We wonder if he knows. If he doesn't, we are certainly not going to be the ones to tell him.

We arrange a posy of flowers for a thank you gift, with the message, "I am grinning from ear to ear". Some more 'thank you' flowers go out to a teacher from a small boy who has been struggling to learn his colours. He helps his mum choose the flowers and decides there must be one for each colour of the rainbow. He proudly recites these to us.

Late in the day, Jennifer is serving a regular customer, Dr Stow, who we know is quite hard of hearing. She cheerfully shouts her questions to him, and it is only as he leaves the shop, looking slightly puzzled, that we all realise it is not Dr Stow at all.

flower shop secrets
GARLANDS

Some customers like to buy plain garlands which they then decorate themselves. Sprigs of ivy, hypericum and holly can be wired into the pine, although always leave the holly until last, otherwise you will get pricked as you wire other things in. Ribbon, pine cones, slices of dried fruit and bundles of cinnamon sticks also work well.

Woolly hats and hearts

Cold
Hands
Warm
Heart

The School Christmas Fair

If you travel north out of Tisbury you climb a steep hill, go through the woods and then down into the village of Chilmark. The village school, built in the same soft grey Chilmark stone as Salisbury Cathedral, sits on the small high street opposite the stream that runs through the village.

I have very fond memories of the school as both my daughters started there when they were five years old. I can still remember all the pancake races, maypole dances, summer sports' days, harvest festivals and nativity plays we attended.

The school often buys flowers from us for staff birthdays and celebrations, so when we hear they are holding a Christmas fair we are pleased to provide a prize for the raffle. I choose leucodendrum, rosy hypericum and Cherry Brandy roses for their bouquet.

Visiting the fair I am reminded of when I bought the hand-made cards and decorations that the girls had prepared in class. In our Christmas box we still have a few cotton-wool snowmen and jam-jar lanterns they made.

In the wendy house some elf and reindeer costumes are hung up ready for the school play.

Winning the Raffle

Mrs Cockrean is almost as pleased to win the flowers. Mrs Cockrean teaches at Chilmark school, but lives in Tisbury. She comes into the shop to buy flowers for friends and is now delighted to have a bouquet of her own.

Clementine's Christmas

This has been a busy year for one of our customers, Clementine. Earlier in the year we helped prepare the flowers for her wedding and now, as Christmas approaches, she opens the doors of her new business.

We bring along some posies of flowers to help decorate her new shop ready for the launch, and also a good luck bouquet from her parents-in-law. Clementine is sat on the floor amongst the boxes and tissue paper unpacking the last of her stock. There are pretty leather-bound notebooks, beaded bags, china bowls the colour of ice cream and crisp white linen pillow cases. I spot a watch nestling in a box of stripy ribbons, each of the ribbons can be used as a watch strap. A perfect present for Libby.

Christmas Shopping

The shops were full of flimsy things,
Like bags she didn't need.
Rings that she could do without,
Face-creams that might mislead.

So this year, he had got it right,
He'd listened, like she said.
He'd bought her something useful,
But sadly, now he's dead.

And if you wish to visit him,
The plot is clear to tell.
His gravestone is an ironing board,
It marks the place he fell.

Clementine's Clementines

Clementines make a bright, Christmas display especially if they still have their original, dark green foliage. If they don't have their leaves you can always add some fresh bay leaves to the bowl for decoration.

Clementines also look good piled on top of fir cones in an open wire basket.

On the Fifth Day
of Christmas

Our plant-man, Jodie, cannot get his lorry under the bridge into Tisbury, so every Monday he calls Ted and she goes to meet him between the railway station and the fields.

She loads up her truck with trays of azaleas, cyclamens, jasmines, roses and orchids. Special orders, such as large box trees, are also collected.

flower shop secrets
AZALEAS

Azaleas enjoy a drop of tea (without milk!) so, if you have some spare, tip it into the container you stand your azalea in for watering.

Back at the shop we are making up a number of orders. One is for a little girl who is off school sick. It is from her father who is away serving in the army. The message is, "get better soon, missing you, Daddy xxx". It is not our only call from the army that day. A brigadier has just remembered his secretary's birthday and on the way into work calls by in his official car. After he leaves we decide we rather like men in uniform visiting the shop.

Ted and Jenny start loading Ted's truck ready for a large wedding we shall be working on over the next few days. We called in some extra help, including Ted's son, Jack, and his friend, Mike, who will be moving some of the heavier plants and arrangements for us. They will also be making tea, but we haven't told them this yet.

A Winter Wedding

Working in the marquee across the lawn from the house, there are pedestal arrangements and large table centres to be made up. The theme is based around white and green and arrangements are to include traditional English blooms mixed with more tropical flowers. This reflects the family's love of the West Indies where they also have a home.

The day starts grey and wet with strong winds. But by the afternoon the skies have cleared and the bridegroom and his friends come out for an impromptu game of rugby on the lawn.

It takes many hands to lift the arrangements safely into place.

flower shop secrets

ORCHIDS

We place a candle in a vase of water in which we also float orchid heads. Orchids like being in a lot of water and it is possible to submerge a whole stem in a tall vase which has been filled to the brim with water. This looks spectacular, especially with lighting behind the vase.

The tables are set and rose petals are scattered on the tablecloths amongst the vases and glasses. Looking at the place names we recognise one of the guests attending the wedding. Maxine is a frequent visitor to the shop and last summer we arranged flowers for her special birthday party. We place a rose petal in each of her wine glasses and add a few extra for good measure around her place.

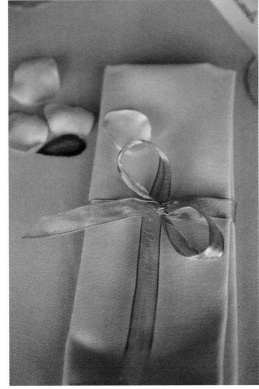

The bridegroom's mother and the rest of his family are clearly enjoying the whole occasion and everyone pitches in to help where they can.

The chefs have arrived and the final preparations are well under way.

Decorating the House

I have fallen in love with this house, particularly the flower room which is stacked with an interesting array of pottery and glass vases. On the table there are a number of bowls planted with narcissi and orchids. I have always dreamt of having a house with a flower room and this one even has a white butler's sink. I wonder if they would notice if I moved in here!

Pink, cream and burgundy pedestal arrangements flank the entrance to the main hall and staircase. Further inside the house we can hear the sound of conversation and laughter.

The colour theme is carried through to the library with smokey hydrangeas and Cezanne roses.

I am ridiculously pleased to see a copy of my first book on the stool in the library and cannot resist taking a photograph of it.

Decorating
the Church

The wedding is to take place at four o'clock, by which time it will be quite dark. The arrangements in the church include roses, veronica and euphorbia and also a considerable number of candles to add to the light and atmosphere.

A gospel choir arrives and is welcomed by the local vicar. Later we hear that the bride walks out of the church to the choir singing "signed, sealed, delivered, I'm yours".

"And on her lover's arm she leant,
And round her waist she felt it fold,
And far across the hills they went
In that new world which is the old."
Alfred Tennyson

Finishing touches

Jennifer finishes decorating the archway leading into the churchyard and the lantern is lit.

Ted lights the lanterns that are hung on shepherd's crooks lining the path to the church door.

Ribbons in a Row

To help place flowers in a large rectangular or square vase, ribbons can be tied in a criss-cross pattern around the vase, as if it were a present.

The stems can then be arranged in the gaps, helping you to get a secure, even spread of flowers.

On the Sixth Day of Christmas

A box of sweet smelling mimosa arrives. A lady who is in the shop at the time wonders if it would be wicked to treat herself to some. We assure her it wouldn't. She recalls how, as a young woman, one of her father's curates brought her back a bottle of mimosa perfume from the south of France and since then she has had a fondness for it.

I am reminded of this story a few days later when a French Christmas market visits the nearby town of Shaftesbury. On one of the stalls there are fragrant pastel coloured soaps made from lavender, peaches and mimosa.

The local primary school delivers a poster for our window advertising their Christmas coffee morning.

I have been told that if you listen carefully, animals receive the gift of speech on Christmas Eve.

A lady arrives at the shop with a calculator, "I believe this is yours". We had been wondering where it had gone and had even turned the bins out as this is where we usually sweep scissors, pencils, staplers and calculators along with the cuttings. This time I had managed to wrap the calculator up in cellophane and deliver it with her bouquet!

Posies for friends and flowers for Ted

London Flowers

Visiting London near Christmas I make sure our journey travels past a number of flower shops and flower stalls. It takes me back to when I had a small shop in south London. Every Monday morning I would head for Covent Garden in my blue and white van and then, still very early, I would drive through the quiet city streets to visit the offices that we had prepared flowers for. Next, it would be back to the shop for bacon sandwiches with Kim and Trish who worked with me.

It was wonderful to work with Kim and Trish who were both far better florists than I was, having worked in places such as The Ritz and Harrods. Trish would laugh and tell us how, when there was a famous film star staying in the hotel, they would walk through the corridors carrying flowers and appearing busy, so they could have a good look.

When the business got bigger we were joined by our own, flamboyant delivery driver, Barrington Wiltshire. We knew him as Barry, but in the evenings he was known to his fans as the DJ, 'Fresh'. We loved Barry, who never let us down, whether he was delivering to the East End of London or to Buckingham Palace.

I call in to see a friend, Nicola, who manages a small, stylish flower shop near The Strand. She is just parcelling up a bouquet of roses, white nerines, cream cabbages and sandy-coloured alstromeria ready for delivery. She wraps it in chocolate brown tissue paper before placing it in a bag that she then ties up with brown ribbons.

flower shop secrets
NICOLA'S SECRET

When choosing flowers for a special event, such as a wedding or party, always include something seasonal; that way, whenever the flower is in season you will be reminded of this occasion.

Nicola tells me they have just finished decorating the adjoining hotel for Christmas. In the main reception area they used pots and pots of amaryllis piled in a huge cone shape to resemble an enormous Christmas tree. Large, natural trees with white lights have been hung by the main door to the hotel from the balconies above.

Now it is time for some shopping.

We wander through the original Covent Garden with its labyrinth of shops and craft stalls. In the sunken courtyard the buskers are entertaining the crowds.

The rain starts to drizzle softly and we head into an Italian café for coffee and cakes. From inside we watch the cars and buses pass, their lights reflected in the wet streets. Blurred by the rain, illuminated taxi signs merge with the Christmas lights and decorations in the shops opposite.

Back to the Country

Back in Tisbury the work in the shop is becoming hectic and we need a constant supply of fresh foliage for our arrangements. Robert, a retired school teacher who has a small-holding by the river, brings us bundles of viburnum, ivy and holly.

Robert is a lovely man and we are enormously grateful for his kindness and help. Although I have a sneaking feeling his frequent visits may also have something to do with Jennifer, as it seems he is becoming increasingly fond of her.

Foliage

"Then, when maid and man took places,
Gay in winter's Christmas dances,
Showing in their merry faces
Kindly smiles and glistening glances"
William Barnes

One of Robert's relatives was William Barnes, a famous local poet and a good friend of Thomas Hardy.

A local bride requests an informal bouquet that is made up of contrasting foliage tied up with raffia.

Eucalyptus

Eucalyptus is wonderfully fragrant and as it dries and keeps its shape well out of water it is suitable for aromatic wreaths and garlands. Although, be warned, you need a lot of stems of eucalyptus to achieve a full look. We also use it for Christmas arrangements that are silvery and white as it complements these colours and its long stems make it ideal for use in larger bouquets of lilies or long-stemmed roses.

Bay

Bay is one of my favourite foliages. I love its sweet, slightly smokey smell and its dusky green colour. Like eucalyptus it dries well but be careful not to hang it where it can be knocked as the leaves get brittle and will snap. If you have a large bay tree or shrub you can cut long stems of it, which makes creating a garland so much easier.

Pine

When the first pine arrives in the shop with its evocative fragrance I know that Christmas is here. We use pine in all types of arrangements, although as the stems are often thick a lot of time can be spent cutting and shaping the ends so they will pierce the Oasis easily. For this reason, and because I think mixing a number of foliages gives depth and texture, I often use the pine sparingly.

Vibernum

With its deep green foliage and pretty white flowers vibernum is a good choice for Christmas arrangements and posies. It is also a shrub that many people seem to have in their gardens so it is often readily available. I particularly like it mixed with deep purples and reds, as this is very Christmassy, but it is a little different. As vibernum can have very bushy stems the small pieces can be cut short to fill in gaps in an Oasis arrangement.

Step by Step

This arrangement can be made using any attractive wide-necked glass vase or bowl.

Step 1: Line the vase with moss and add your soaked Oasis that has been cut to fit.

Step 2: Take pieces of florist's wire that have been bent and cut and tape these to the end of the candle with Oasis tape. This will help secure your candle in the Oasis. An alternative is to use a ready-to-go candle holder.

Step 3: Arrange your foliage around the candle. We have used a mixture of vibernum, ivy and pine.

Step 4: Thread wire through and around the bottom part of a pine cone, twisting the ends together to form a single spike that can then be poked into the Oasis.

Step 5: In a similar way thread a wire into the edge of two slices of dried orange and add these to the arrangement.

Dried Oranges

I have read of many different ways to dry orange slices, so I thought I would try some to see which worked best. I tried a conventional oven, a fan assisted oven, in the Aga, on top of the Aga and in the airing cupboard.

The best result was on a cake rack on top of the Aga but this was closely followed by using a fan assisted oven on the lowest possible heat. This also works well with limes and lemons.

Of course, you can always let someone else do it for you and buy a bag of chunky Christmas pot-pourri and then your orange slices will smell fabulous too.

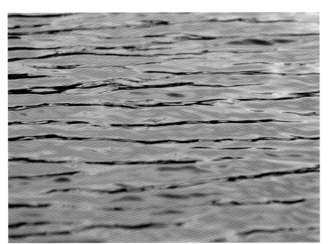

On the Seventh Day
of Christmas

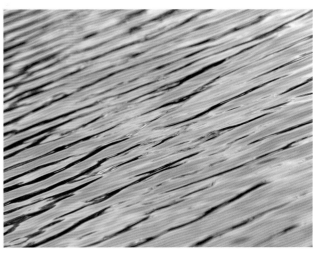

On a Cold and Frosty Morning

With so much to be done it is an early start for us all. As I drive to work, the sun is just rising over the silver white countryside and the dew has frozen into crystals in the hedgerows.

I can barely get the door of the shop open as the delivery has already arrived. The crates are stacked high, filled with wraps of flowers, trays of bulbs and bundles of pine. Resting on these I can see the scarlet of poinsettias peeping out of the top of two tall boxes.

I catch Jennifer drawing a Christmas tree on the window as she clears the condensation.

Ted turns the heating up and puts the kettle on. I tie my apron strings and pull the sleeves of my jumper as far down over my hands as I can. We work our way as fast as possible through the boxes, cutting and conditioning the flowers, and then check through the stock that is already in the shop. Once the empty crates are stacked away I pause for hot chocolate and a croissant with apricot jam before starting on the orders.

"These winter nights, against my window-pane
Nature with busy pencil draws designs
Of ferns and blossoms and fine spray of pines,
Oak-leaf and acorns and fantastic vines"
Thomas Bailey Aldrich

The vicar comes in to find a volunteer to read one of the Christmas lessons at the carol service. Ted and I look very busy and it is soft-hearted Jennifer who agrees to do it, even though she is obviously terrified at the thought of it. I promise I will go along on the night to support her.

The evening of the carol service turns out to be very cold and there are icy blasts of snow and sleet in the air as we make our way through the village. Robert has walked with Jennifer to the church and chats to her encouragingly. The service is packed and when her turn comes Jennifer reads her piece clearly and well. The choir sing a number of carols, including a solo by our Saturday girl Rosie, who we find has a beautiful voice.

An early visitor to the shop orders "a small bouquet for a tiny lady who is turning 100" – I have a vision of this lady disappearing under a sea of flowers if the bouquet is too large.

Ted takes down details for flowers that are to be presented to those who have helped with a local pantomime. However this is a pantomime with a difference. It is called "Snow White and the Seven Forwards" and it is being performed by members of the local rugby club.

There is a flurry of orders that seem to be connected with animals. One poor lady is recovering after being chased by a bull when she was out walking; she was saved from serious injury by her dog who defended her. Another lady sends flowers to her neighbours, apologising because her goat had escaped and eaten their shrubs.

A daughter calls by to send her mother flowers because today is the day her horse has to be put down. She writes a personal note to her mum to go with the flowers.

We take a delivery of flowers down the valley to Manor Farm to help decorate the farmhouse for a shoot lunch. In the huge, flag-stoned kitchen Gillie is preparing a joint of their own beef for the meal. She has already taken home-made soup, fruit cake and sloe gin up to their guests on the downs.

The Shoot Lunch

It is easy to locate Manor Farm as there are two regimental badges cut into the chalk hillside that can be seen from miles away. These badges were made during the First World War by soldiers who were training nearby, before being sent to the Front.

Like many in the area, farmers Richard and Gillie have had to think of new ways to make running the farm worthwhile. Gillie now rents out two of their cottages for holiday lets and Richard, who is also a blacksmith, is the first person we turn to if we need something made, like shepherds' crooks for hanging lanterns.

The table is set and the fire is lit. As the smell of cooking wafts through from the kitchen I wish I could pull up a chair and stay for the afternoon.

One of Gillie and Richard's frequent house guests is a young man called Rob. Rob is the son of family friends and over the years he has helped Richard to renovate cottages and to bring in the harvest. He has also eaten Gillie out of house and home and occasionally driven them both mad. Now this is all forgotten as he has bought Gillie a present of a delivery of flowers, once a month for a year. Very attractive and boyishly charming we, of course, think Rob can do no wrong.

Gillie is another person who is keen to offer help when we are looking for more foliage, such as holly and ivy.

flower shop secrets
BERRIES

This year the holly bushes are laden with berries, but in years when they are scarce we use artificial berries wired around the holly sprigs. If the rest of the arrangement is full and natural no one notices that these berries are not real.

The Holly and the Ivy

"So now is come our joyful feast,
Let every man be jolly;
Each room with ivy leaves is dressed,
And every post with holly."
George Wither

Visiting Bee

Driving up Tisbury High Street on my way home I love glancing in the window of Bee's cottage to see the large country kitchen and cheerful log fire.

When Bee first came into the shop I thought I recognised her, but this may well be because she is an actress and I had watched something she had appeared in. Nowadays, she tells me, she spends a lot of her time working with Laurence Olivier's son training other people.

*"Winter is the time for clear cold starlight nights,
And driving snows, and frozen roads and rivers,
For crowding round the blazing Christmas fire,
For telling tales that make the blood run cold,
For sipping elder-wine and cracking filberts,
For friendships, chilblains, fun, roast beef, mince pies,
And shivering fits on jumping into bed:
And thus the year goes round, and round, and round."*
James Hurnard

I call by with a trug filled with pine, deep purple anemones, cabbages, cinnamon sticks and satsumas.

Ted's Mulled Wine

Pour two bottles of red wine into a saucepan. Slice two oranges and add these to the saucepan, along with eight cloves, one cinnamon stick and four tablespoons of brown sugar. Simmer for at least ten minutes making sure you do not boil the mixture. Sprinkle with nutmeg before serving.

Some people like to add some water to the mix and others, like myself, like to add a splash of Cointreau.

On the Eighth Day of Christmas

Jenny takes an order from a lady whose mother has a passion for eighteenth century art. For her birthday party her family has hired rooms in London that date back to that time. She tells us the staff dresses in period costume and that you can almost hear the swish of silk skirts coming down the stairs. We are to prepare flowers in rich gold, green and burgundy colours.

One of our favourite customers rings us to explain that he is going to dinner with his boss and he knows his "sparkling conversation will not be enough to impress" – could we prepare an extra special bouquet for him to take.

In conversation with a customer buying some china for a Christmas present I hear how she works in the flower room at a hospice. She tells me that they receive many arrangements from funerals that they then dismantle and make into bedside posies and table centres. I am pleased to think that the flowers go on to be enjoyed by other people.

Ted's son, Sam, is in the shop helping and we keep him busy clearing the windows, removing the rubbish and delivering flowers that are within walking distance.

With so many orders being prepared the raffle-ticket book is brought out and we number both the order and the arrangement to ensure all the flowers get to the right home. We are running short of buckets to store the flowers in and I notice that some Champagne buckets I lent Ted for her husband's birthday party have been commandeered into service.

Christmas is
The colour of spruce and dogwood,
The shape of bells and plum pud,
The smell of spice and firewood,
And Gran still up to no good.

A Time to Remember

Sadly, winter is often a time for funerals, and these seem to be especially poignant at Christmas time. We are asked to prepare a natural spray of flowers for a lady who loved her wild and scented cottage garden, whilst a young woman wants to take a single flower for her friend who died very young. She tells us how they used to put a single flower under the windscreen wipers if they saw each other's car parked in town.

Other tributes include personal messages sent through the flowers and foliage that are chosen. One gentleman asks us to include a branch from an olive plant in with the flowers.

Christmas is also a time for memories. A man in his early thirties rushes into the shop and enquires if we can make up a wreath for him. He asks if this can be done quickly as he is only down for a short visit. Later we learn that this young man has visited his best friend's grave every year since he tragically died when they were playing together as ten-year-old boys.

Another wreath is required for a local writer's relative who fought in the war and received the Victoria Cross but whose grave was never marked. Many years on John has organised a ceremony with the backing of the army to commemorate his uncle's life.

"In this short life that only lasts an hour,
How much – how little – is within our power"
Emily Dickinson

We are contacted by an interior design company that is decorating a famous footballer's house for Christmas. They ask us to prepare a large pine door wreath threaded with gold and plum coloured ribbon. They are very discreet and will not tell us the name of the footballer, but it doesn't stop us trying to guess.

An elderly gentleman buys a wreath we have ready for sale in the shop. It has been decorated with pine cones, holly and cinnamon sticks. "Are those cigars?" he enquires, pointing at the cinnamon. I think he is quite disappointed when we explain that he shouldn't try smoking them.

When you have made up dozens and dozens of door wreaths and it gets to be too much, you can always put one on your head and pretend you are the Statue of Liberty!

flower shop secrets
TABLE CENTRES

If you don't have time to make a table decoration take a door wreath and place it in the centre of the table with a church candle in the middle.

Step by Step

Step 1: Take a shallow dish filled with water and add lots of stems of foliage that you have cut quite short. Here we have used holly and ivy.

Step 2: The mass of foliage will now hold the flowers in place. First we added lisianthus, then tulips, again, both cut quite short.

Step 3: In between the flowers we poked sprigs of wax flower.

Step 4: Finally, we added some dried orange slices that we simply placed in amongst the flowers.

Jennifer's Cheese Straws

This is Jennifer's quick, easy (and I know from experience) very tasty recipe for cheese straws. She buys a pack of puff pastry which she rolls out. She then sprinkles it with grated cheese and a little garlic salt. Sometimes she adds a touch of Marmite rather than the garlic salt. Folding the pastry so all the ingredients are caught inside she rolls the pastry out again.

Cutting the pastry into strips she then twists them and arranges them onto a greased baking tray. These are then cooked in the oven at gas mark 6, 400°f (200°c), for 15 minutes or until golden brown.

On the Ninth Day of Christmas

> "A reeling road, a rolling road, that rambles round the shire,
> And after him the parson ran, the sexton and the squire"
> **G K Chesterton**

An always welcome customer, Amanda, comes into the shop. We have not seen her for some time as she has been suffering from a very bad back. When she leaves she has a ready team of volunteers to take her parcels to the car for her.

We receive a request for a table arrangement to be sent by overnight courier to a family as a Christmas gift. As the family has young children I am asked to make it suitable for them as well. I raid the Christmas chocolates that we keep on the counter by the till and have a great time tying these in amongst the flowers.

Some customers bring in Christmas gifts for us to enjoy in the shop, such as wine and cakes. One of our customers, John, brings us biscuits throughout the year. Now he appears with an extra special box of chocolates.

Up and down the road the shops are decorated ready for Christmas. The girls at the hairdressers have made a wonderful gingerbread house out of sweets and biscuits.

A lady from Denmark comes to the shop to order some Christmas arrangements and a large bunch of tulips. She explains that in Scandinavia it is a sign of good fortune to be given tulips at Christmas.

There is a superstition that red and white flowers are unlucky and some customers do avoid this combination. I rather like the mixture and think, at Christmas, paper-whites tucked in amongst red anemones can look very festive.

A Scandanavian Christmas

Kim, who used to work with me in my flower shop in London, came from a Swedish family and she was the first person to introduce me to the ribbons, hearts and wooden decorations that we associate with a Scandinavian Christmas. Every year I put a wooden branch of lights in my window that Kim brought me back from Sweden many years ago.

Once upon a time, long ago, there was a kind nobleman who had two daughters. After his wife died, leaving the family in despair, the poor man fell upon hard times. The family had to move into a peasant's cottage where the daughters did their own cooking, sewing and cleaning.

One evening after the daughters had washed out their clothes they hung their stockings over the fireplace to dry. That night Saint Nicholas, knowing the despair of the father, stopped by the nobleman's house. Looking in the window Saint Nicholas saw that the family had gone to bed. He also noticed the daughters' stockings. Inspiration struck Saint Nicholas and he took two small bags of gold from his pouch and threw them one by one down the chimney so they landed in the stockings.

Christmas on the Farm

Crafts on the Farm

My friend, Carolyn, and her husband, Peter, run a dairy farm in the next valley and it is from here that Carolyn runs her jewellery business. She trained in London but now, with children and a farm to keep her busy, she works from home, selling her jewellery at fairs and at the 'open house' that she usually runs at Christmas.

I visit the farm to bring Carolyn some flowers and to help her set out the goods. Snow is forecast and the sky is slate grey but we are hopeful that it will stay clear until the evening.

flower shop secrets
FRUIT

Flowers do not like being near fruit, so at Christmas, when there are bowls of fruit and nuts on display, make sure your flowers are not standing next to them.

I am reminded of Carolyn every day, as it was she who designed and made my eternity ring which was a surprise Christmas present two years ago. Looking at her new designs I cannot resist buying a silver bookmark as a Christmas present for my best friend, Pip.

As a silversmith and goldsmith Carolyn has her own hallmark, which makes her work especially personal and special for me.

This year Carolyn has been working with other local crafts people, many of whom I met at a recent open evening. I put aside a picture from Gaynor Ringland who makes beautiful textile pictures. She is also a talented glass artist.

Chatting to potter Ed Duckworth, he describes how he likes studying medieval paintings and re-creating the shapes and forms he sees in them. One large pottery jug looks ideal for tulips, or even red wine.

Festive Vases

Chunky vases are often good for displaying candles at Christmas and these can be made to look more festive simply by putting some natural decorations in the base.

Good ideas include pine cones, nuts, dried fruit and berries.

On the
Tenth
Day of
Christmas

The days turn very foggy and Jennifer and I drive at a snail's pace as we head over to Shaftesbury to help decorate a customer's house for Christmas.

Earlier in the day a lady had been in to buy flowers for her friend who may not be able to get a flight home to Canada for Christmas because of the fog. Another couple was in the village buying flowers and extra food and drink for their parents who cannot fly out to board their Christmas cruise. The grandchildren had been busy decorating the guest room for them and I noticed they still had paint and glitter in their hair. They were determined to make it a merry Christmas for them.

Our customer Jane's house is set on a hill looking over the Blackmore Vale and in better weather has stunning views. Jane likes her arrangements to be quite striking and dramatic to suit the large rooms with their wooden flooring and panelling.

Jane is one of our friendliest customers and one of the first things she does on our arrival is to pour us each a glass of red wine.

The kitchen fireplace is hung with a garland of eucalyptus through which white lights are threaded. Aubergine-coloured stars are hung amongst the branches.

Jennifer works on the table in the entrance hall filling a glass and iron vase with amaryllis, eucalyptus and twisted willow.

flower shop secrets
FIREPLACES

Garlands dry out very quickly over a fireplace so an alternative is to line up a number of arrangements so they look like a garland. In this case five large zinc containers are filled with Oasis and ivy and then strung with Christmas lights and hung with stars.

The Christmas Tree Festival

In the village church the Christmas tree festival is underway. Local groups and businesses come in to decorate a tree, directed by the choir master, Mr Power. Food and mulled wine have been laid on and the atmosphere is warm and jolly.

*"When Christmas bells are swinging above the fields of snow,
We hear sweet voices ringing from lands of long ago"*
Ella Wheeler Wilcox

The Tisbury bell ringers hang their tree, rather appropriately with bells, and then pull it high up onto the church wall.

Two young girls help the village accountants, Wood & Co, to get their numbers right.

The junior choir has a musical tree complete with home-made choir boys and girls.

The children from the Sacred Heart Catholic church show their colourful support for an orphanage in Peru.

Red and white wooden toys deck the branches of the Tisbury Pre-school tree.

I recognise one of the ladies in the church as a customer who had been in the shop earlier. She is part of an amateur operatic group and they have ordered a bridal bouquet for a forth-coming performance.

One of my favourite trees has been decorated by the local hardware shop which has been hung with paintbrushes dipped in glitter.

In the centre of the church is the prayer tree. Underneath the tree there is a basket of tags and pencils for people to write their personal Christmas prayers and wishes.

My daughters have come to help me decorate a tree for the flower shop. Of course it has to be decked with flowers. We also add gingham bows and candy-canes.

Our Christmas fairy is given a mini gerbera to hold, turning her into a flower fairy.

flower shop secrets
TEST TUBES

Test tubes filled with water are really useful if you wish to hang flowers amongst greenery and keep them fresh. They are also good for thick-stemmed flowers, like hyacinths, that can be tricky to push into Oasis. Sometimes it is easier to place a few test tubes into the Oasis and then add the flowers to the tubes.

Every year the girls and I each choose a new decoration for our Christmas tree. After the box of baubles has spent a year in the loft it is lovely to unwrap all the different well-loved choices we have made over the years.

This year I cannot resist some wacky Irish flower fairies that are made in a workshop in the woods near Galway. Each flower fairy comes with a packet of flower seeds that I am certain I will forget to plant in the spring.

"Every moment her light was growing fainter; and he knew that if it went out she would be no more. Her voice was so low that at first he could not make out what she said. Then he made it out. She was saying that she thought she could get well again if children believed in fairies."

Sir J M Barrie

Out making a delivery one morning I meet an elderly lady who has a beautiful garden which she invites me to look round. At the bottom of the garden I am enchanted to find a tiny house which I am sure must be for the fairies. I am glad that it is not just the young who believe in fairies. Although perhaps I should not be surprised; my father, who is eighty, still firmly believes in Father Christmas. Quite right too.

"Deep within the winter forest among the snowdrift wide,
You can find a magic place where all the fairies hide"
Anon

Crispy Puddings

These are good fun for children to make, although they may need you to help them lick the bowl.

First melt some chocolate in a bowl over a saucepan of water and then pour in your rice crispies. Spoon the mixture into muffin cases and put somewhere cool to set.

Roll out some fondant icing and cut into splodgy shapes. Drape these over the cakes and decorate with red and green writing icing.

On the Eleventh Day of Christmas

Amy, a sweet and friendly young mum, is in the shop organising flowers for Christmas gifts. As Jennifer serves her I take a call from her partner. Knowing she is here he asks me to make a bouquet for Amy, to be presented to her before she leaves the shop.

It seems to be a day for romance. A young man comes in and buys six of our loveliest roses for his girlfriend. They are not supposed to be giving each other presents as they have just returned from a special weekend in Paris, but he cannot resist buying her something. We apologise a little as these sumptuous roses are quite expensive, but he says it doesn't matter as, "she is worth every penny".

A teenage boy calls in. He is in my daughter Alex's year at school and I have known him since he was short and very grubby, although I don't remind him of this. He wants to give his girlfriend some flowers as they have been going out for six months. He plans to take them into school in his backpack so we make sure they are securely packaged for him. My daughter tells me later that he braves his friends' ridicule and gives them to her in front of all his classmates. "Mum," she says, "all the girls cried."

A father and his sons come in to buy a year's worth of flower deliveries as a Christmas present. The first delivery is to be sent on Christmas Eve.

We prepare some buttonholes of roses and thistles for a Scottish bridegroom and his ushers. They tell us there is to be a piper playing outside the church and I am reminded of a wedding I once attended in St Andrews. My friend, not knowing what to buy his brother for a wedding present, organised a kilted and uniformed pipe and drum band to march into the reception as a surprise gift. What he did not know was that the bride's father told her before he died that whenever she heard the pipes and drums he would be with her.

meet me under the mistletoe!

it's christmas

An elderly gentleman comes in to buy flowers and mistletoe for his wife as it is their wedding anniversary. We offer them our congratulations but he claims we have got it wrong and that we should really be offering her our sympathy!

flower shop secrets
MISTLETOE

Take some mistletoe berries and rub them into the fork of a tree in your garden. This imitates the action of a Mistle Thrush and may well be the beginning of your own mistletoe crop.

Jenny kissed me

"Say I'm weary, say I'm sad,
Say that health and wealth have miss'd me,
Say I'm growing old, but add,
Jenny kiss'd me."
Leigh Hunt

And the Shepherds Came

A delivery is sent to London at the request of a very proud grandmother. After much anxious waiting her first grandchild, Liberty, has been born. She is pleased to tell us that her daughter and the baby are doing well.

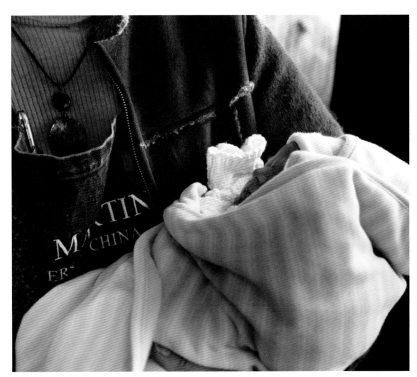

We hear from another grandmother who tells us of one of the proudest moments she has known. She was going to visit her pregnant daughter and, as she drew up outside the house, she was dismayed to see an ambulance with flashing lights parked there. When she rushed inside she found that her daughter was about to give birth and had not had time to get to the maternity hospital. By her daughter's side, reassuring and remarkably relaxed, were the ambulance men. They confided to her the reason they were so at ease was that both their fathers had been shepherds.

Baubles and Biscuits

Hannah and Simon live with their small daughters on the beautiful 10,000 acre Fonthill Estate which Simon manages for the owner Lord Margadale. On a grey and wintry morning I deliver arrangements of roses and berries for Hannah, who is getting the house ready for their Christmas guests.

Simon's parents are travelling down from Lincolnshire and his sisters will be joining them from their homes in Brighton and Bath.

There is the smell of cooking in the kitchen and on a cooling tray are biscuits Hannah, Rosie and Isabella have made to hang on the Christmas tree. Hannah was trained as a cook and used to run her own catering business – it looks like the girls are taking after their mum.

CHRISTMAS BUNNIES

The tree has been brought in from the forest on the estate and the girls empty the box of decorations onto the floor, pulling out the baubles and strands of tinsel.

A little girl's Christmas

Pink sugar mice and silk lilac bows,
Trains up to London and matinee shows.
Glitter and sequins in hair and on floors,
Secrets and wrapping and firmly closed doors.
Dancing with grown-ups that lift me up high,
A flash of red ribbons that twirl as I fly.
Signing my name on cards and on tags,
Biscuits and cakes from boxes and bags.
The smiling white angel we hang on the tree,
Soft woollen stockings for Alex and me.
Dreaming of fairies in tales long ago,
Silent soft darkness as down falls the snow.
Christmas Eve comes and I'm tucked in crisp sheets,
Wishing for dolls and sugary treats.
Mind full of sleigh bells ringing out in the cold
Tell Father Christmas I'll never grow old.
Never too old for these angels of white
Or my parent's soft touch as they kiss me goodnight.
Libby Page

With the girls so little, Hannah has given up her catering business and is concentrating on her other love, painting. Working from home she takes commissions for portraits and animal paintings.

The tree is decorated and the lights are lit. Christmas is almost here. Hannah tells me they are planning a very special Christmas lunch for their guests as they intend to hold it in the old lodge that sits in the middle of the deer park on the estate.

Rosie tucks baby Jesus in

Hannah's Cookies

Hannah tells me the trick to making biscuits with a good clear shape is to put the dough in the fridge before you roll it out and cook it.

Mix together 10 oz of plain flour, 4 oz of unsalted butter, 3 oz of dark brown sugar and some ground cinnamon. In another bowl beat together 2 eggs and 3 tablespoons of runny honey. Gradually add this to the first bowl until it forms a dough.

Once the dough has been chilled in the fridge roll it out and cut it into shapes, placing them on a baking tray lined with greaseproof paper. Cook for around 20 minutes at gas mark 3, 325°f (170°c).

On the Twelfth Day of Christmas

The last few days before Christmas are the busiest and by now we are all very tired. Sometimes we even struggle to get the right words out. Ted asks me to pass a "bick blag" for the rubbish, and a customer and I struggle to remember the name for Oasis, "you know," she says, "the green asbestosy stuff".

Friends call by for flowers and to wish us a happy Christmas. My friend, Fiona, comes in ready to fill her house with flowers; she is a bit fed up as she has just been put on strong antibiotics so she will not be able to enjoy a drink over Christmas. "So Christmas starts here," she decides.

Businesses nearby hold lunches and Christmas parties and we are asked to prepare a number of thank you bouquets. One of the directors of a local business sends his secretary a large bouquet as a thank you "for all the things you quietly do".

The Tisbury firemen are all local men, who in addition to rushing out for emergency calls, hold down other jobs as well. On the last Saturday before Christmas the firemen are out in the High Street raising funds. Who could resist them?

Step by Step

Decorating a mantelpiece can be very easy with masses of greenery and a few special flowers.

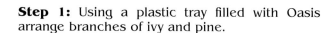

Step 1: Using a plastic tray filled with Oasis arrange branches of ivy and pine.

Step 2: Add your flowers. Odd numbers work best.

Step 3: Securely tie or wire in crystals so they hang down from the arrangement and catch the light from the fire.

Step 4: Add thin candles or tapers to the arrangement by poking them firmly into the Oasis.

Christmas in the Village Pub

After a long day in the flower shop I call into the Beckford Arms to rest my aching feet and toast myself by the fire. And if a friend wishes to buy me a large glass of red wine, that is very welcome too.

Earlier in the day the Beckford's manager was in the flower shop buying amaryllis, eucalyptus and twisted willow. I see that she has created a wonderful arrangement with them in one of the cosy alcoves of the pub.

*"Let now the chimneys blaze,
And cups o'er flow with wine;
Let well-tuned words amaze
With harmony divine"*
Thomas Campion

Fire and Ice

I am chatting to Winston, the Beckford's chef, about photography and flowers when he asks me how many vases I think he has. My guess of around 20 falls way short, as he tells me he has 480 vases at home. It turns out that Winston is a glass collector and has a special passion for the Scandinavian period, sometimes known as Fire and Ice.

Later that week Winston brings some vases into the pub to show me. They are from the Finish glass company Riihimaki and over the years Winston has collected them from car boot sales and junk shops.

Santa Comes to School

Broadchalke School is a regular customer of ours and it is always a pleasure to call in with deliveries for them. As I walk through the playground I am reminded of a comment from one of our other customers – she said it doesn't matter where you are in the world, a school playground always sounds the same.

The teachers in the staff room are bubbling over with barely contained excitement. Today Father Christmas is coming to visit the school. The staff has spent all morning converting the brightly lit school library into a cosy grotto for Santa.

They take me along the corridor to see it, closing the door quickly on the curious children passing by. As I am admiring their hard work we hear two small voices outside. "I can hear someone in there ....I think it's Father Christmas."

"And then, in a twinkling, I heard on the roof
The prancing and pawing of each little hoof.
As I drew in my head, and was turning around,
Down the chimney St. Nicholas came with a bound.
He was dressed all in fur, from his head to his foot,
And his clothes were all tarnished with ashes and soot"
Clement Clarke Moore

A few years ago Broadchalke School suffered from a fire which swept through the building. Since then they have successfully raised funds to help the school move to a new site. Parents, pupils and teachers joined the fund raising, with auctions of promises, literary evenings and cakes sales. The headmistress tells me that one of their fathers even threw himself out of a plane for them.

Countdown to Christmas

2 3 4 5
8 9 10 11
14 15 16 17

We used our hands and feet to make these reindeer.

"Only three people got out of the 11.54. The first was a country woman with two baskety boxes full of live chickens who stuck their russet heads out anxiously through the wicker bars; the second was Miss Peckitt, the grocer's wife's cousin, with a tin box and three brown-paper parcels; and the third –
'Oh! my Daddy, my Daddy!' That scream went like a knife into the heart of everyone in the train, and people put their heads out of the windows to see a tall pale man with lips set in a thin close line, and a little girl clinging to him with arms and legs, while his arms went tightly round her."

Edith Nesbit

Family and Friends Coming Home

We are often asked to prepare flowers and decorations for guest bedrooms when customers have family and friends coming to stay. Here we have created a bay swag for above a bed and planted white cyclamen into matching baskets. With leftover branches of bay we decorate the picture frames.

"She tells her love while half asleep,
In the dark hours,
With half-words whispered low:
As Earth stirs in her winter sleep
And puts out grass and flowers
Despite the snow,
Despite the falling snow."
Robert Graves

flower shop secrets
ROSES

If roses are becoming overblown and look like they might be wilting re-cut them and push them further into your arrangement. The surrounding flowers and foliage will help hold the rose's shape for a bit longer.

Crimson spray roses are mixed with ivy, alstromeria and burnt orange freesia to complement the raspberry and faded gold colours of this bedroom.

Posies and parcels for a pale blue and cream bedroom.
White anemones are arranged with pink lisianthus,
roses and thistles.

Christmas is Coming
(and the Goose is Getting Fat)

Now there are the last few things to be done. The visit to the butcher, the firewood to stack and the last pieces of holly and ivy to be gathered.

"Heap on the wood, the wind is chill;
But let it whistle as it will,
We'll keep our Christmas merry still."
Sir Walter Scott

It is the last day in the flower shop before we close for the Christmas holiday.

We are no longer taking orders for arrangements, but the young man who bought his lady six spectacular roses calls by. Could we just make him something as he doesn't want his girlfriend to have the bother … for such a romantic, of course we can.

Everyone is out helping with the deliveries. The doctor, the dog, the hairdresser and the baby!

A friend of Jennifer's calls by and chats about her Christmas plans and how she is looking forward to midnight mass at their village church. She explains that her husband, who is a good organist, is likely to be down the road playing in the Catholic church. She says this makes her chuckle as her husband is Jewish. She is not sure whether the ladies of the church realise this, but they have sometimes complimented him on some of his impromptu melodies which are, in fact, Hebrew airs.

There is Champagne to be drunk and the shop must be cleared of all the last flowers. Ted sends the girls off into the village with the few remaining bunches to offer them to people in return for a contribution to our charity tin.

*"And the rooks in families homeward go
And so do I"*

Thomas Hardy

The shop is swept, the blinds drawn down and the door is shut and locked. With many wishes for a very happy Christmas we all head off in different directions to our homes.

Driving Home

Driving back along the Avenue in Tisbury I pass an amazing display of Christmas lights. Filling these gardens with decorations is a tradition started years ago by a couple whose granddaughter had cancer. She loved the pretty lights and so her grandparents made a point of creating a spectacular display for her, which the neighbours also joined in with. Sadly, their granddaughter died but they continue to light their garden each year for other children in the village to enjoy.

Coming Home

If you leave a light in the window,
I will turn from the road to you.
The moon will light the familiar fields
And the path where the snowberries grew.

Touching the edge of shadowy trees,
On the trail that no woodman clears.
Fossil leaves pressed deep in the moss,
Soft steps passing like years.

The fox buried deep in Winter's hedge,
Will watch with unblinking eye,
As the sounds scurry into the silence,
And the owl's wing brushes the sky.

Florists are often the last ones to decorate their own homes so it is only on Christmas Eve that I add the finishing touches to the fireplace. You will find florists rarely make garlands for themselves but are very good at arranging branches on a mantelpiece to look like a swag!

Bowls are turned upside down to raise the candles away from the wood and then cinnamon sticks, ribbons and other decorations are simply placed in amongst the branches. Finally a few short pieces of foliage are poked in to hide the bowls and the candles are lit.

"It is time to enjoy yourself,
It is later than you think"
Chinese Proverb

Vases of Chocolates

I must admit I stole this idea from my friend, Nicky. When I walked into her house I saw she had emptied a couple of tins of chocolates into a large glass vase on the hall table. It looked so colourful and inviting.

Vases also look good filled with the baubles that cannot be fitted on the Christmas tree.

You will find the colour combination changes as the family eat their way through the chocolates until you are left with the ones no one likes. As this varies by household I have always thought it would be a good idea to swap these at the end of the holidays. Imagine somebody not liking orange creams.

Waiting
for
Father
Christmas

"And I heard him exclaim as he drove out of sight,
Happy Christmas to all and to all a goodnight!"